The Library of NATIVE AMERICANS

The Iroquois
of New York

Greg Roza

The Rosen Publishing Group's
PowerKids Press™
New York

For Myrna, my grandmother

Published in 2003 by The Rosen Publishing Group, Inc.
29 East 21st Street, New York, NY 10010

Photo and Illustration Credits: Cover, p. 51 courtesy David Oestreicher (p. 51 photograph by Steven Steinberg); p. 4 Erica Clendening; p. 6-7 © Ashmolean Museum, Oxford, UK/Bridgeman Art Library; pp. 8, 11, 12, 17, 20, 29 courtesy of the New York State Museum, Albany, NY; pp. 18, 22, 24, 27, 30, 33, 40, 42, 44, 47 courtesy, National Museum of the American Indian, Smithsonian Institution (p. 18, P14082; p. 22, S040404, photo by Pam Dewey; p. 24, S012823, photo by Karen Furth; p. 27, N22322, photo by DeCost Smith; p. 30, T135376, photo by Pam Dewey; p. 33, T179689, photo by Gina Fuentes-Wallker; p. 40, N41484; p. 42, T216857, photo by Pam Dewey; p. 44, S18492, photo by Pam Dewey; p. 47, S029611, photo by Pam Dewey); p. 34 © Ewing Galloway/Index Stock Imagery, Inc.; p. 36 Lee Snider/CORBIS; p. 38 Old Military and Civil Records, National Archives and Records Administration; p. 39 © Hulton Archive/Getty Images; p. 52 © Ted Spiegel/CORBIS; p. 55 © Reuters NewMedia Inc./CORBIS.

Book Design: Erica Clendening

Roza, Greg.
       The Iroquois of New York / by Greg Roza.
              p. cm. — (The library of Native Americans)
       Includes bibliographical references and index.
       Summary: This book describes the history, culture, government, and current situation of the Haudenosaunee, Native Americans who have been referred to as the Iroquois.
       ISBN 0-8239-6425-6
       1. Iroquois Indians—History—Juvenile literature. [1. Iroquois Indians. 2. Indians of North America—New York (State).] I. Title. II. Series.
       974.7004'9755—dc21

Manufactured in the United States of America

There are a variety of terminologies that have been employed when writing about Native Americans. There are sometimes differences between the original language used by a Native American group for certain names or vocabulary and the anglicized or modernized versions of such names or terms. Although this book contains terms that we feel will be most recognizable to our readership, there may also exist synonymous or native words that are preferred by certain speakers.

Contents

The Six Nations of The Iroquois Confederacy

Lake Ontario

Oneidas

Onondagas   **Mohawks**

Cayugas

Senecas

Lake Erie

New York

North Carolina

Tuscarora

One

Introducing the Iroquois People

The people of the Iroquois Confederacy lived on the land that is today known as New York State. The Confederacy was a union of the Mohawk, Oneida, Onondaga, Cayuga, and Seneca peoples, all of whom shared a similar language and culture. These five tribes became known as the League of the Five Nations after agreeing to live together in peace. In the early 1700s, the Tuscarora nation—originally from North Carolina—joined the Five Nations, and the Iroquois Confederacy became known as the League of the Six Nations.

The peoples of the Iroquois Confederacy call themselves the Haudenosaunee (ho-dee-no-SHO-nee), which means "people of the longhouse." The word Iroquois actually refers to a language spoken by many different groups of Native Americans. The Haudenosaunee do not like to be called Iroquois, because it is the French pronunciation of an Algonquian word that means "real snake."

The Haudenosaunee were known for being fierce warriors, and few Native Americans dared to oppose them. The Haudenosaunee stood in the way of European expansion in North America for hundreds of years. They were also fair and

This map shows the territories of the five New York Iroquois nations, along with the sixth nation, the Tuscarora, who were from the area now known as North Carolina.

diplomatic people. It was diplomacy that helped them to form the League of the Five Nations, and allowed it to flourish.

The Haudenosaunee are well known for many reasons. Their most notable contribution to American history and culture is the constitution of the Iroquois Confederacy. Originally created to keep

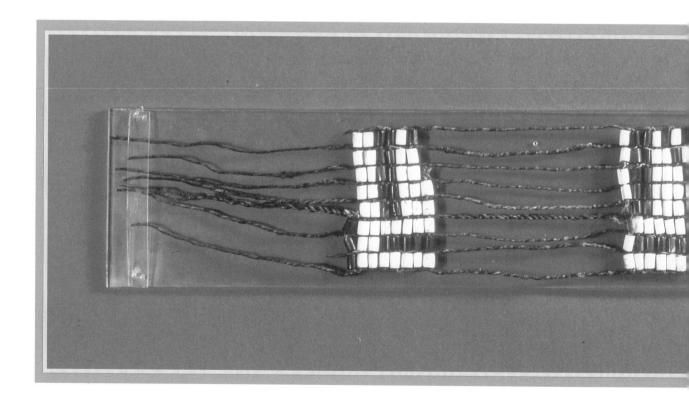

6 This wampum belt is decorated with shell beads and was probably made in the seventeenth century. The Haudenosaunee made wampum belts to use in special ceremonies, give as gifts, or record special events.

peace among the Haudenosaunee, the constitution created an efficient and innovative form of government that inspired a young United States. Many elements of Haudenosaunee culture helped to shape American culture: foods, games, clothing, language, art, and everyday activities.

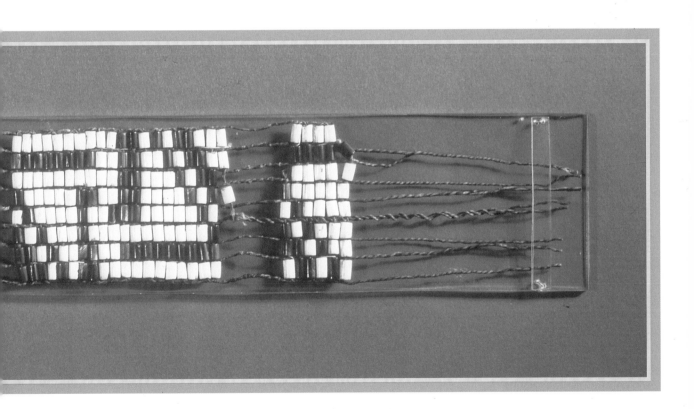

Two

Early History of the Haudenosaunee

The Haudenosaunee may have settled in the Northeast as early as the twelfth or thirteenth century. No one really knows how they came to occupy the area that is today known as New York State. They may have drifted north by way of the St. Lawrence River or the Mississippi River. Others think they may be the descendants of ancient tribes that lived in the woodlands of the Northeast.

The Haudenosaunee were surrounded by Algonquian peoples. The Algonquians are a group of Native Americans who speak related languages. The Algonquian and the Haudenosaunee did not always get along, and they frequently fought throughout the years. The Haudenosaunee were able to survive among so many enemies for two reasons: They were a diplomatic alliance, and they were strategic warriors.

Algonquian peoples were not the only Native American groups with which the Haudenosaunee fought. They fought with just about every group within their reach, including other Iroquoian nations. After the Iroquois Confederacy was formed, the Haudenosaunee encouraged surrounding Iroquoian nations, including the Huron, Susquehannock, Erie, and Neutrals, to join them. These nations either joined the Confederacy of their own will or were forced by the Haudenosaunee to join. If they did not join the Confederacy, the Haudenosaunee would wage war with them.

This carving decorated a clay pot that was made by the Mohawk nation in the late 1500s.

Dangerous Living

Before the Iroquois Confederacy was formed, daily life for the Haudenosaunee was violent and dangerous. Many people lived in fear. There were few alliances between nations in those years, and feuds were frequent, cruel, and long lasting. Even within nations, there was little safety. Warriors achieved fame and importance with each battle, and few cared to stop fighting.

One of the most feared warriors was a cruel man named Tadodaho. Tadodaho was an Onondaga chieftain, and he ruled his people with fear and bloodshed. Most people believed that he was a sorcerer who could kill his enemies and others who disagreed with him without even being present. Not only did he threaten the people of his own nation, but he also scared people of the Cayuga and Seneca nations as well. At first, fear of Tadodaho and other chieftains like him kept the Haudenosaunee from achieving peace between the nations.

Messengers of Peace

There were two men who wanted peace among the Haudenosaunee more than anything. They would not let Tadodaho scare them. One was a Wendot (or Huron) man living with the Mohawk nation. His name was Deganawidah. He came to the land of the Haudenosaunee when his own people rejected his message of peace. Deganawidah had come to the Mohawks from the Wendot Nation north of Lake Ontario. The Mohawks were known to be powerful warriors, but were kind to their own members. The Mohawks welcomed him into their tribe, but they tested him to make sure that he was the one who was destined to bring peace to the Haudenosaunee. Most people refer to Deganawidah as "Peacemaker" or "The Man from the North" out of respect for this great man.

The Iroquois chipped stones to make arrow points and leaf-shaped knife blades.

The other peaceful man was an Onondaga chieftain, as was Tadodaho. His name was Hayenwatha. Unlike Tadodaho, he wanted to bring peace to his people. Hayenwatha was a great orator, and he begged the Onondaga to stop fighting. Many people agreed with his desire for peace, but Tadodaho continued to harass the Onondaga. One by one, Hayenwatha's three daughters died of

This replica depicts an Iroquois longhouse surrounded by a protective wall.

sickness. The people of the Onondaga Nation were convinced that it was the evil work of the sorcerer Tadodaho. Hopes for peace among the Onondaga were crushed.

The deep emotional pain caused by losing his beloved daughters caused Hayenwatha to flee into the wilderness, where he wandered alone for a long time. Upset over his loss, Hayenwatha was no longer sure what he was supposed to do. The natural world eventually soothed his sorrowful mind. Hayenwatha wandered close to a Mohawk village, and several women noticed him sitting peacefully nearby. He was wearing a necklace of white shells, which they recognized as a sign of peace. The Mohawks told Peacemaker about the strange man, and Peacemaker immediately welcomed Hayenwatha into the village. Peacemaker consoled him, easing his intense sorrow.

Hayenwatha was adopted into the Mohawk Nation just as Peacemaker had been. Together, Hayenwatha and Peacemaker sought to spread the messages of peace and unity to all the nations of the Haudenosaunee. Their message became known as the Great Peace. The Mohawk was the first nation to accept the Great Peace.

The Iroquois Confederacy

Hayenwatha and Peacemaker wanted to form a confederacy, or family, of Iroquois nations connected by a common desire for peace. Once the Mohawk Nation had accepted the Great Peace, Hayenwatha and Peacemaker traveled to other Haudenosaunee nations and asked them to join the Iroquois Confederacy, also called the Iroquois League. The Oneida and Cayuga happily accepted the message of peace. Hayenwatha and Peacemaker had difficulty convincing the chiefs of Onondaga and Seneca to join the Confederacy.

Those who were reluctant to accept the Great Peace were convinced in a number of ways. It is believed that Peacemaker and Hayenwatha used spiritual powers to convince Tadodaho to accept their message of peace. Tadodaho and other chiefs were promised positions of power and importance in the newly formed family.

No one is sure when the Iroquois Confederacy began. Some experts say that it started around 1550, while other experts and many of the Iroquois people believe that it began as early as 1142. The Onondaga Nation became the meeting place for all Confederacy councils, or government meetings. Each nation was guaranteed equal representation within the Iroquois Confederacy.

Nations were made up of smaller groups called clans, or groups of relatives who could be traced back to a single female ancestor. Haudenosaunee society was matrilineal. This means that a family's heritage was traced back through the oldest living female. The leaders of the clans were called chiefs. Together, clan chiefs helped to govern the nations to which they belonged. Clan chiefs automatically became Confederacy chiefs. This ensured that each nation, and each clan in that nation, had a representative in the Confederacy. It also ensured that each clan and nation would be free to continue practicing its own traditions. Each nation was allowed to keep its culture intact, and no one was forced to give up his or her preferred way of life. This kept the people of the Iroquois Confederacy happy as the League grew stronger and more unified.

Symbols of the Iroquois Confederacy

Most Haudenosaunee lived in longhouses. Entire families lived in these lodges made of wood and bark. The Iroquois Confederacy was thought of as a family, and the Iroquois longhouse became a symbol for that family. The Mohawk Nation became known as the "keepers of the Eastern Door" of the house, and the Seneca were the "keepers of the Western Door" of the house. The Onondaga were at the center of the Iroquois Confederacy, and they became known as the "keepers of the Council Fire." All meetings took place at the Onondaga village in the center of the longhouse.

The pine tree, or "Tree of the Great Long Leaves," also became a symbol for the Iroquois Confederacy. A pine tree was symbolically planted in Onondaga territory and was said to have four roots spreading out in all directions: north, south, east, and west. Any nation that wished to join the Iroquois Confederacy only had to follow one of the roots to find the tree. An eagle sat on top of the tree searching for danger and protecting the League. A hole at the foot of the tree was filled with weapons as a sign of new peace.

The Iroquois Confederacy Grows

Once the Confederacy was established, it grew quickly. Other Iroquoian nations were urged to join the League to make it stronger and to help protect the Haudenosaunee from enemies. As the Iroquois Confederacy developed, the Haudenosaunee quickly became known as fair and diplomatic people. Many nations gladly joined the Confederacy. Others rejected the offer to join the league of nations. Although the Haudenosaunee were fair and diplomatic, they also kept peace within the League by eliminating threats from enemy tribes.

Because of their great sense of diplomacy, as well as their growing might, the peoples of the Iroquois Confederacy were able to control a very large area of land: roughly from Virginia to Ohio, and from southern Canada to Kentucky. By creating the Iroquois Confederacy, Peacemaker and Hayenwatha created one of the most powerful and influential Native American groups in history.

As this model shows, a typical Iroquois village consisted of several longhouses. Each longhouse measured between 50 and 100 feet long.

Three
Daily Life

Daily life in a Haudenosaunee village was busy. The men hunted, made tools, built and fixed shelters, and protected their families. The women farmed, gathered wild foods, cooked, made clothing, and took care of the children. The children played most of the day. The adults, too, found time to play games. During the winter months, when it was too cold to go outside, families told stories around the fire.

Farming and Gathering

The Haudenosaunee thrived by performing the daily survival activities that had been handed down from their ancestors with skill and confidence. Over the years, they perfected their skills in hunting, farming, healing, and the construction of tools necessary to carry out daily tasks. Surviving in the woodlands of the Northeast was not always easy, but the Haudenosaunee and the Iroquois Confederacy flourished in part due to their day-to-day survival skills.

Haudenosaunee women were farmers. They invented a system of growing three crops together in the same plot of soil. First, the women planted corn. When the corn was tall enough, they planted

A group of Haudenosaunee men were photographed during their trip to meet the governor of New York. Three of these men wear clothing designed in the style worn by Native Americans who live on the plains. The second man from the left wears a traditional Iroquois headdress.

beans and squash in the same soil. The vines of the beans and the squash covered the ground, keeping the soil moist. The Haudenosaunee thanked the Creator for giving them these three important vegetables. Together they were known as the "three sisters." They were also known as "the supporters of life." The importance of these three vegetables was celebrated many times during the year in thanksgiving celebrations. When the soil could no longer support the "three sisters," the men would clear a new plot of land and build a new village.

In addition to farming, women also gathered wild berries, nuts, plants, and roots for food. The Haudenosaunee especially liked wild strawberries; they even had a special celebration once a year to thank the Creator for them. The women also made maple syrup in the spring.

This model shows Haudenosaunee women gathering food. The most important crops that they harvested were corn, beans, and squash.

Hunting

Haudenosaunee men spent much of their time hunting. The men were adept with a variety of weapons: bows and arrows, blowguns, spears, and even clubs. Over the years, they developed crafty methods of chasing down their prey. Sometimes they chased an animal into a lake, where it would be easier to catch. The men often left the village in late fall to go hunting and returned in midwinter. In the spring, they caught fish with spears and bows and arrows. Some even made hooks and lures to catch fish.

They hunted a variety of animals, such as bear, moose, and small woodland animals. The most commonly hunted animal was deer. The Haudenosaunee used deer for food and also used their hides for clothing and their bones and antlers to make tools. Just as with the "three sisters," the Haudenosaunee were grateful for everything the Creator gave them. They did not want to take advantage of the Creator's generosity, so they never hunted more animals than they needed.

Weapons and Tools

Haudenosaunee men made bows from soft wood. Arrowheads, spear points, and knives were made from sharpened rocks, such as flint and slate. War hammers were made by setting heavy, round stones in carved wooden handles. The men made most of the tools used by the Haudenosaunee. They made farming tools from wood, stones, animal bones, and antlers. They made knives and ax blades from sharpened stones. Animal bones and antlers were sharpened and used as awls to punch holes in tough animal hides. Spoons and bowls were carved from wood. Canoes were built with wood and tree bark.

The Haudenosaunee crafted bowls, such as this medicine bowl, from wood.

Healing

Medicine men and women (also called healers or shamans) used a variety of methods to cure the sick and to care for the injured. They were skilled in the use of plants and herbs as medicines. They also knew how to set broken bones, dress wounds, and even perform some kinds of surgery.

The Haudenosaunee believed that sicknesses were caused by natural as well as magical causes. Evil spirits and sorcerers were known to make people sick. Because of this, many Haudenosaunee healers used magic arts to heal illnesses, create remedies, and perform medical procedures. Chants, spells, dances, and sacred instruments were used in healing rituals. Healers were believed to have sacred knowledge, making them very important and revered members of Haudenosaunee society.

Adoption

In order to preserve their numbers, the Haudenosaunee frequently adopted members of enemy nations who had been taken prisoner. Some of these prisoners were sacrificed in the name of supernatural powers, while others became full-fledged citizens of the Haudenosaunee. This practice allowed the Haudenosaunee to replenish their populations and helped them to remain a large, powerful force.

Longhouses

The Haudenosaunee lived in rectangular homes called longhouses that were between 50 and 100 feet long. These houses were made of wood, covered with elm bark, and had openings on both ends. The Haudenosaunee often made holes in the roofs where the smoke from their fires could safely escape. Fifteen to twenty related families lived together in a single longhouse.

Cooking and Food

The women used a variety of methods for preparing meals. Food was boiled in clay pots, roasted over open fires, or made into soups. Corn was often dried and ground into cornmeal, which was then used in a number of recipes, including cakes that were similar to tortillas. Meat was often smoked and stored for the winter months in containers made of tree bark.

The Haudenosaunee had a creative way of preparing corn. First, they boiled the dried corn with wood ashes, which made it easier to remove from the cob. It also made the corn more nutritious. Then they poured the corn into woven baskets called hulling baskets. The hulls were removed from the softened kernels of corn, which was called hominy. Hominy, corn, and beans were often combined to make a dish called succotash.

The Haudenosaunee used mortars and pestles to grind some foods.

Clothing

Haudenosaunee women made clothing with the hides and furs of the animals that the men caught. They tanned the hides so they were soft but strong. Using sharpened awls to punch holes in the hides, they sewed the hides together with thread made from plant fibers. They made shirts, sashes, bibs, pants, dresses, and moccasins this way. The women decorated the clothing, especially the shirts and moccasins, with porcupine quills, and eventually with glass beads after Europeans arrived in North America and began to trade. These pieces of clothing could take a month or more to make, but each was a work of art. The women also made headdresses and headbands from leather, beads, corn husks, and feathers. Today, the Haudenosaunee refer to this traditional style of clothing as regalia. Regalia is usually worn only for special festivals and traditional ceremonies.

Men and Women

Men and women in Haudenosaunee society had clearly defined roles. The men were the hunters, protectors, and builders. Women cooked, farmed, gathered wild foods and herbs, made clothing, and raised the children. The women owned everything but the weapons. Women held their families together and made sure everyone helped each other with tasks. They also named the babies. Although men assumed the roles of leadership within the Iroquois Confederacy, women traditionally chose the council leaders. They also had the power to "dehorn" a leader, or remove him from his position, if they felt that he was not doing his job.

Even though the Haudenosaunee society was matrilineal, no one really had power over anyone else within a nation. All people were treated as equals. Each member of a nation had his or her own responsibilities, and everyone worked to make life as good as possible for all.

Clans

Extended families were called clans. Clans were named for particular animals (Bear, Wolf, Turtle, and so on). The oldest living female relative was the head of each clan. Whole clans lived in a single longhouse. Marriages were not permitted between people of the same clan. When a man and a woman married, he moved into her clan's longhouse, but remained a member of his own clan. Sometimes outsiders who had abandoned their nations or who had been captured during battles were adopted by a clan. They became full citizens of the clan's nation.

In the Iroquois society, women were responsible for raising the children. This photo was taken on an Onondaga reservation in 1888.

Children

Babies and toddlers stayed with their mothers all day long. Women carried their children on their backs in sturdy cradles while they gathered food, worked in the fields, and made food. Children would stay in their cradles most of the time, until they were able to walk by themselves.

Young children were allowed to play all day long. The boys played with toy versions of adult tools and weapons. They also wrestled and hunted small animals. By age eight or nine, boys brought home small animals, such as rabbits, for meals. By the time they were teenagers, the boys went along on hunting trips to watch and to learn from the men. The girls watched their mothers cook food and make clothes and learned from them. As they got older, girls helped to take care of the younger children and joined their mothers in the fields. These leisurely childhood activities prepared children for adult responsibilities when they came of age.

Children were never reprimanded for their actions. Instead, the adults used fables of monsters and evil spirits to make them behave. These stories were sometimes based on scary creatures who wandered the wilderness looking for children to eat. These stories took the place of punishment in Haudenosaunee society.

Recreation

Stories were also used as education and entertainment, particularly during festivals. Designated members of each clan remembered long stories of the clan's history, traditions, ceremonies, and fables. Sometimes, these stories were tens of thousands of words long and were remembered with precise accuracy. Stories taught children about their heritage and customs. They also kept people entertained during long winter months inside the longhouse.

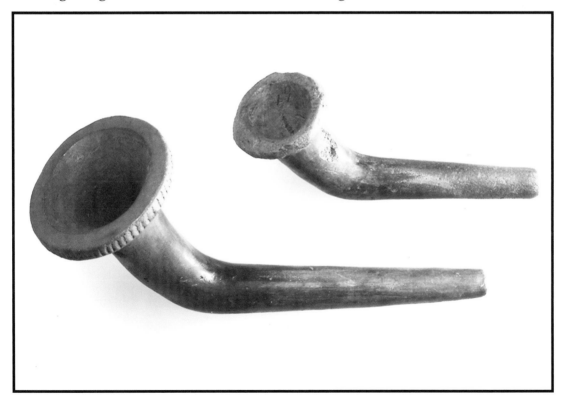

The Haudenosaunee made pipes from clay. These pipes were for personal use, while more decorated pipes were used in religious ceremonies.

Adults and children liked to play games when they had time. Children often played games that mimicked adult chores and duties. The women played a game similar to hockey. The men played a game called "snow snake," a contest to see who could slide a long spear the farthest along a groove made in the snow.

The Haudenosaunee made moccasins from animals' hides and decorated them with porcupine quills and beads.

Lacrosse was, and still is, a very important game for the Haudenosaunee. Each lacrosse player carries a special racket with a long handle and a net used to catch and to carry a small, hard ball. Two teams strive to get the ball past their opponents and into a goal. Haudenosaunee men played this game for recreation, but it was also used for ceremonial and political purposes. When two nations had a dispute, they sometimes settled it with a game of lacrosse. The winner of the game would be the winner of the dispute. A lacrosse game like this could have as many as twenty people on each side and could last for many hours. Sometimes the games became violent, and injuries were common. Some spectators liked to bet on the games. Lacrosse games were also considered a good way to train men for war. The players talked about strategy and tried to outwit and overpower their opponents.

Wampum

Wampum were long strings or belts made of white and purple shells. Since purple shells were less common, the more purple shells a wampum belt had, the more important or valuable it was. Wampum were used for a variety of reasons. They were used in special ceremonies. They were given as gifts of honor, or to finalize an agreement or contract between nations. They were also used as "invitations." Council chiefs were called to meetings with wampum belts. The chiefs brought the belts with them to prove that they were invited.

Sometimes wampum were made to record history or special events. These belts were then "read" by people trained in wampum symbols. Some wampum belts are very famous. The Hiawatha Belt recorded the union of the first five nations under the Iroquois Confederacy. At the center of this belt is a pine tree, the symbol of the Iroquois Confederacy. The rectangles joined to the tree represent the nations that the League united. The Hiawatha Belt is made almost entirely of purple shells, which shows how important it is to the Haudenosaunee. This wampum belt has become a priceless artifact, recording the most important event in Haudenosaunee history.

When Europeans arrived in North America, they quickly realized how important wampum were to the Haudenosaunee. They did not understand wampum's role in the Haudenosaunee culture, however, and mistook the belts for money. In fact, some Europeans even started duplicating wampum and used them as one of the first forms of currency in the New World. The Haudenosaunee never used wampum as currency.

The clothing that the Haudenosaunee wore was beautifully decorated by patterns made with beads.

33

Four
Encounters with Europeans

The Haudenosaunee had been living in the area known today as New York State for more than 400 years before Europeans arrived. In creating the Iroquois Confederacy, they had formed a powerful and an influential union of Haudenosaunee people. But when Europeans arrived, the Haudenosaunee's world would change.

Europeans started coming to North America in the late 1400s. They came for numerous reasons. Jamestown, Virginia, was the first permanent European settlement in North America. These people came to find riches. The Pilgrims landed in Plymouth, Massachusetts, hoping to attain religious freedom. Both of these groups formed friendly relations with Native Americans.

The first Europeans that the Haudenosaunee met were the French. Before they met French explorers and settlers in the early 1600s, the Haudenosaunee owned French products through trade and warfare with Algonquian-speaking nations. They were particularly eager to acquire metal knives, metal axes, and cloth brought to North America by the French.

The Mohawk began raiding Algonquian and even other Haudenosaunee villages to the north for more French products. This disrupted the French and Native American fur trade. In

This painting by Ewing Galloway depicts the pilgrims arriving from England in Massachusetts. When the Europeans and Native Americans came into contact with each other, both groups changed forever.

response, a French leader named Samuel de Champlain led an attack against the Mohawk. Mohawk warriors were stunned by the presence of the Europeans, whom they had never seen before. The French easily defeated the Mohawk forces with their musket

rifles. This encounter was just the beginning of a long and violent history between the Haudenosaunee people and the French settlers.

The Mohawk soon formed a close connection with Dutch, and later British, settlers along the Hudson River. The Haudenosaunee traded furs for numerous objects, including metal pots, knives, axes, cloth, beads, and rifles. This helped to strengthen the Iroquois Confederacy against the Algonquian nations and French settlers to the north. The Haudenosaunee stopped the French from extending their fur trading south of Lake Ontario. The five nations of the Iroquois

Samuel de Champlain was the French leader who helped the Algonquian protect their fur trade from the Mohawk. The statue of him pictured here stands on Nepean Point in Ottawa, Ontario, Canada.

Confederacy were strong and unified, and they controlled a large and an important stretch of land. The nations of the Iroquois Confederacy attacked neighboring tribes who traded with the French, gaining even more land in their vast empire. With the help of the British and their rifles, the Iroquois Confederacy reached a new height of military strength during this time.

Between the years 1689 and 1763, the Haudenosaunee and the British were involved in a series of wars against the Algonquian nations and the French. The last of these wars was known as the French and Indian War, and it lasted from 1754 to 1763. The British eventually won this war, and the French were once again driven out from Haudenosaunee land.

Revolutionary War

After the French and Indian War, British and Haudenosaunee bonds grew stronger. A Mohawk chief named Thayendanegea, also called Joseph Brant, became very close to several key British leaders. When American colonists rose up to fight for their independence from England in 1775, Joseph Brant asked two Seneca chiefs, Red Jacket and Cornplanter, to help the British win the Revolutionary War. Brant convinced them that the American colonists posed a greater threat to the Iroquois Confederacy than did the British. The Onondaga and Cayuga nations also joined the British. However, the Tuscarora and Oneida nations decided to back the American colonists. This represented the first significant rift between the nations of the Iroquois Confederacy since it was first established. Haudenosaunee nations raised arms against each other, marking a sad time in their history.

The colonists won the Revolutionary War in 1783. Now that the British could no longer help and protect the Haudenosaunee, the nations were at the mercy of American forces. General George Washington ordered troops to burn the villages of the nations that had fought against the colonists.

Haudenosaunee people were relocated to designated areas of land called reservations. Some groups fled the American soldiers to regions as far away as Canada, Wisconsin, and Oklahoma; some Hau - denosaunee people still live in these areas today.

At Fort Stanwix in 1784, the six Iroquois nations signed this treaty with the United States, giving them a small section of western New York.

Thayendanegea, or Joseph Brant (1742–1807), was a Mohawk chief who was
educated by the British and convinced several Iroquois nations to oppose
America's fight for independence.

The Haudenosaunee were very spiritual people, and religion filled their everyday lives. Their traditions, stories, songs, and even day-to-day activities, such as hunting and farming, were structured around their spiritual beliefs. They believed in a noble Creator who made everything in their world, including plants, animals, the Sun, the Moon, wind, water, earth, fire, and the Haudenosaunee themselves. They also believed that everything in their world—from plants and animals to the wind and the water—had a spirit. Some spirits, like the Creator, were kindly and righteous. Other spirits were evil, and they sought to disrupt the Haudenosaunee way of life. Much of the Haudenosaunees' spiritual lives were spent giving thanks to kind and helpful spirits, and warding off evil spirits.

Sky Woman

The Haudenosaunee creation story is a very important part of their culture. It explains where they came from. It also explains why the world is filled with animals, plants, and other natural objects. While there are several versions of the Haudenosaunee creation story, they all tell a similar story.

A Cayuga chief named Red Cloud was photographed in traditional clothing. His headdress is a bonnet type preferred by the Cayugas and Senecas.

41

In a time long before the Haudenosaunee existed, there was a place called the Sky World. This magical place was somewhere beyond the skies. Magical people lived there, including a powerful being known as the Sky Chief and his young wife, Sky Woman. Sky Woman was going to have a baby. One day, while collecting seeds and berries, Sky Woman fell into a deep hole near an uprooted tree. The world below the Sky World was a vast ocean. As she fell, the birds of this world felt sorry for her and caught her on their backs. There was no land on which to set her down, so sea creatures hurried to create a place for her to live. Muskrat dove deep into the ocean and came back with a handful of mud. Muskrat placed the

This needle case was made of black buckskin and decorated with quills.

mud on Turtle's back, and this grew until it became Earth. The seeds and berries that Sky Woman had been collecting in Sky World became the plants of Earth.

Sky Woman soon had a daughter. When the daughter grew up, she gave birth to male twins, one good and one evil. The evil one forced his way out his mother's side and killed her in childbirth. Sky Woman buried her daughter, and from her body grew the plants that the Haudenosaunee call "the three sisters" or "the supporters of life": corn, squash, and beans.

As the twins grew, they began to compete with each other. The good twin created majestic animals, medicinal plants, and beautiful scenery. The evil twin created sicknesses, evil spirits, and monsters. But the evil twin was not strong enough to destroy the good twin. The good twin then created the Haudenosaunee, so that others could enjoy his beautiful creations. This is how the Haudenosaunee believe they were created.

Sacred Rituals

The Haudenosaunee have many sacred rituals. Just as they do their creation story, they take these rituals very seriously, and they are often cautious about sharing them with people who are not Haudenosaunee. This is because not everyone understands how important they are in the Haudenosaunee culture, and because some people do not show the proper respect for these beliefs.

One such ritual was performed by a group called the False Face Society. Twice a year, a group of men wore scary and colorful masks made of wood or corn husks. They believed that these ceremonial masks gave them supernatural powers. They walked around the village and into homes, scaring away evil spirits that caused sickness and disease. The rest of the people thanked them and gave them gifts and food. When the ceremony was over, the only female member of the False Face Society would hide all the masks until they were needed again. To the Haudenosaunee, these sacred masks are a vital part of their religion. They do not like it when the masks are put on display for people outside of their society. They are offended when people refer to the masks as "crafts" and when they are imitated for non-religious purposes.

Giving Thanks

The Creator gave life to the Haudenosaunee, as well as a beautiful world filled with life-sustaining creatures. For this they were very thankful and showed their gratitude in many ways. They were also very thankful for the benevolent acts of spirits inhabiting their world. The Haudenosaunee worshiped the

One type of weapon that the Haudenosaunee carried when they went to war was a wooden club such as the one pictured here.

world around them and everything in it, seeking to establish a positive relationship with the world of nature and its numerous spirits. When hunting, for example, Haudenosaunee men would thank the animal's spirit for giving itself to them so that they could survive.

Thanksgiving ceremonies were an important part of the Haudenosaunee culture. Each nation celebrated a number of events every year, including ones that honored such agricultural developments as planting and harvesting. The frequent celebrations helped to unify the community. People ate lots of delicious food, danced, sang songs, and played instruments. Babies were named during these celebrations. First and foremost, however, they held these rituals to thank the Creator for being kind to them and to chase away evil spirits. The Haudenosaunee often thanked the generous spirits of plants, animals, and other things in nature: birds, trees, water, crops, even worms. They thanked the spirits of so many things that these rituals sometimes lasted up to three days. Perhaps the oldest and most important thanksgiving ceremony was the Green Corn Festival. This ceremony was held every year at harvest time. The Haudenosaunee felt it was important to thank the Creator for giving them food to survive the winter months. Another important celebration was the New Year's Festival. This celebration was held in midwinter when the men came back to the village from their annual hunting trip. Other celebrations were held to honor the Sun, the Moon, the thunder, the maple tree, the wild strawberry, and many other life-sustaining spirits.

Longhouse Religion

In the late 1700s, the Haudenosaunee—as well as other Native American groups—were faced with a long list of dangers brought upon them by settlers. Americans were taking advantage of Native Americans, even after groups like the Haudenosaunee helped them to win wars and agreed to share the land with them. Native Americans signed treaties that Americans had no intention of honoring. Slowly the Haudenosaunee were being forced into tiny areas called reservations. Americans often bribed Native Americans with alcohol, and some Native Americans eventually became addicted to alcohol. Haudenosaunee beliefs and rituals were being neglected and forgotten. This was a bad time in the history of the Haudenosaunee.

A man named Cornplanter, the chief warrior of the Seneca, felt it was necessary for the Haudenosaunee to work with Americans in order to survive. He had received this message from a group of settlers called Quakers. Quakers were a group of Christians living close to the Haudenosaunee. They believed in hard work, sincere prayer, sobriety, and a stable family. Unlike other white settlers, they had shown great compassion for Native Americans for a long time. The Quakers wanted to teach the Haudenosaunee to read and write, so they would not be taken advantage of by other settlers. They also suggested that the

Haudenosaunee accept the business and agricultural practices of the European Americans in order to survive. Cornplanter urged his people to allow the Quakers to help them in many ways.

Handsome Lake was a Seneca chief, a respected medicine man, and half brother to Cornplanter. Handsome Lake agreed with Cornplanter. Unfortunately, Handsome Lake had fallen prey to alcohol, and his health was starting to fail. One day in 1799, Handsome Lake grew very ill, and many people thought that he was going to die. However, Handsome Lake soon woke up and revealed to the Seneca that he had received an important message from the Creator.

The Haudenosaunee cooked with wooden ladles such as this.

The Creator told him that he must convince the Haudenosaunee to stop acting in evil ways, and that they must remember their sacred traditions. The Creator told Handsome Lake to preach the message of Gaiwiio, which means "the Good Word." He and Cornplanter preached the message of the Good Word, and many Haudenosaunee eagerly listened. Handsome Lake's message spread so quickly and helped so many Native Americans improve their lives that even Thomas Jefferson sent him a letter commending him on his good work.

The Creator's message, revealed to the people through Handsome Lake, became known as the Longhouse religion. It was a combination of the old Haudenosaunee religion and the religion of the Quakers. Those who accepted the Good Word followed sober, spiritual lives, and again began observing old Haudenosaunee celebrations like the Green Corn Festival and the Midwinter Festival. Believers in the Longhouse religion worked hard to combine spiritualism with new agricultural expertise. They also formed a new conviction to become educated in the ways of European American society and culture so that they could benefit. While some Haudenosaunee considered this to be going against tradition, many accepted the Longhouse religion as a way to save their people from extinction. The Longhouse religion is still observed by many Haudenosaunee today.

Tales and Legends

Like all cultures, the Haudenosaunee had many stories that they shared and passed down from one generation to the next. Tales and legends helped the Haudenosaunee to make sense of the world around them. There were stories that explained why the Haudenosaunee needed to respect nature and the creatures they found in it. Other stories told why it was important to be kind to friends, family, and even strangers.

While these stories often served as a form of entertainment, many were used to educate the Haudenosaunee children. Tales and legends instructed children on how to act in society and showed them which behaviors were acceptable and which were not. One of the more popular tales is about a young woman who saw her reflection in a lake. She became so fixated on her own beauty that she neglected her chores. She acted as if the people around her were not as good as she was. Her elders warned her to stop staring at herself and to help out with chores, or else something terrible might happen. She refused to listen to them and continued to stare at her reflection in the lake day and night. One day, she woke up to find that she could not see or speak. The Creator had become so angry with her for being vain and lazy that he took her face away from her.

There was a lesson in this children's story. Being selfish and lazy can have terrible consequences. To further stress this important message, children were taught to make corn husk dolls that had no faces. This was intended to be a reminder that everyone had responsibilities in society, and that the Creator was happiest when everyone worked together.

Art, Music, and Dance

In the Haudenosaunee society, many everyday objects were works of art. The intricate quill and bead work on traditional clothing, for example, often took a month or more to complete. Women wove beautiful baskets and mats from corn husks for everyday cooking use. Men carved ornate spoons from wood. They used clay to make decorative containers and cooking pots. Soapstone and sometimes wood were carved to form beautiful yet functional pipes. Women made delicate combs from animal bones and antlers. Wampum took a long time to make, and each one was an original work of art. Even weapons like war hammers and knives were made with drawings and figures on them. The Haudenosaunee expressed their artistic nature in everything they made.

Music and musical instruments were used for ceremonial purposes and for entertainment. The Haudenosaunee made and played drums, rattles, and sticks. Some instruments, like the snapping turtle rattle, were used only for special rituals. They also sang and stomped their feet in time with the music. Often, one person would lead the song, and then everyone else repeated or answered his or her words.

Dances were also very important to rituals. Types of dances included the stomp, the fish, and the side-step shuffle. The side-step shuffle was a type of dance that was only performed by women.

Turtle rattles like the one shown at right were widely used throughout the Eastern Woodlands. The carved wooden rattle at left also depicts a turtle.

The Iroquois Confederacy lasted for hundreds of years. Early American politicians modeled their new government—a democracy—on the Iroquois Confederacy because of its intelligent and compassionate structure. It would be this same government that would cause the Confederacy's fall from power and prestige. The Revolutionary War tore the Iroquois Confederacy apart. When the war was over, the newly formed American government disbanded the Iroquois Confederacy with treaties. The Haudenosaunee were forced to move to a total of seventeen reservations all over North America, in New York, Wisconsin, Oklahoma, Ontario, and Quebec.

Honoring Treaties

Native Americans all over the United States have been angry with the U.S. government for years. Their homeland was taken from them in exchange for small pieces of land called reservations. Haudenosaunee reservations have shrunk due to the construction of modern highways and dams.

Native Americans are still fighting to have their treaties honored by the American government. Some Native American groups have

A Mohawk man and boy attend a 1974 ceremony in Ontario that commemorated the arrival of loyalist Mohawks to Canada during the Revolutionary War.

met with success, hundreds of years after the treaties were originally signed. The town of Salamanca, New York, for example, is the only U.S. city on native-owned land and is now owned and leased by the Seneca. Many nations have insisted that the U.S. government honor its treaties so that they may raise revenues badly needed by their people. Thanks to the conditions outlined by Native American treaties, Native Americans may sell tax-free products (especially gasoline and tobacco products) and run casinos and bingo halls. They have come to see these business practices as necessary in the struggle to keep their culture and society intact.

Famous and Regular People

Some Haudenosaunee people have achieved fame, especially in the areas of art and entertainment. Jay Silverheels (Mohawk) and Graham Greene (Oneida) are two notable actors. Famous Haudenosaunee also include the acclaimed artist Carson Waterman (Seneca) and the singers and songwriters Joanne Shenandoah (Oneida) and Pura Fe (Tuscarora).

Today, many Haudenosaunee practice the Longhouse Religion and attend traditional Haudenosaunee ceremonies, while many others believe in Christianity. They wear regalia at special times during the year and celebrate their long, colorful heritage as peoples of the Iroquois Confederacy. At these gatherings, they dance, pray, and eat. The Haudenosaunee also continue to make traditional clothing, baskets, tools, and weapons. They sing ceremonial songs and recite historic speeches and stories. Lacrosse is still a very important part of the modern Haudenosaunee culture. The Haudenosaunee are very proud of their traditions and customs, and they have worked hard to keep them alive.

On July 4, 2001, the actor and member of the Oneida nation Graham Greene participated in a celebration of the 225th anniversary of the Declaration of Independence.

Timeline

Between 1100 and 1400	Iroquois-speaking peoples settle in the area that is today known as New York State.
1142 or mid-1500s	The Iroquois Confederacy is founded.
1609	Samuel de Champlain leads French and Algonquian forces against the Mohawk. This is the Haudenosaunees' first encounter with Europeans.
1610	Dutch traders arrive in New York State's Hudson Valley. In the following years, the Haudenosaunee fight with nearby nations for control of trade with Europeans.
1674	The first treaty between the Haudenosaunee and the Europeans is signed. It is between the colony of Maryland and the Seneca Nation.
1722	The Tuscarora Nation joins the Iroquois Confederacy.
1775	The Revolutionary War begins. The nations of the Iroquois Confederacy are torn between aiding the British or the American colonists.

1779	General George Washington sends American troops to destroy the villages of Haudenosaunee nations that fought for the British during the Revolutionary War.
1779	Treaties with the American government disband the Iroquois Confederacy.
1783	The Treaty of Paris ends the Revolutionary War.
1784	The Treaty of Fort Stanwix is signed by the United States and the Haudenosaunee, reducing the amount of land for the Native Americans but allowing them to live there undisturbed.
1794	The Jay Treaty is signed by Great Britain and the United States.
1799	Seneca Handsome Lake has a spiritual vision that leads to the development of the Longhouse religion.
1823	Part of the Oneida nation decides to move west to a reservation near Green Bay, Wisconsin.
1831	Members of the Seneca and Cayuga nations are forced from their homes. They move to the Indian Territory, which would become Oklahoma.
Late 1950s to mid-1960s	Native Americans lose much of their land. The building of the Kinzua Dam causes the Seneca to lose 9,000 acres in southwestern New York and northwestern Pennsylvania. The Tuscarora and the Mohawk lose a large portion of their lands to projects near Niagara Falls and the St. Lawrence seaway.

Glossary and Pronunciation Guide

alliance (uh-LY-uhnts) An agreement between two or more groups in order to achieve a common goal.

ancestor (AN-sehs-tuhr) A relative who lived before you.

chief (CHEEF) A male leader of a Native American group.

clan (KLAN) Groups of Native American relatives who could be traced back to a single female ancestor.

confederacy (kuhn-FEH-duh-ruh-see) A group of people or nations that are united and that share the same beliefs.

council (KOWN-sul) A group of people who gather to discuss laws and rules.

descendant (dih-SEHN-duhnt) A relative who lives after you.

diplomacy (duh-PLOH-muh-see) Skill in dealing with people fairly.

heritage (HER-uh-tihj) An object or a tradition passed down through the generations.

Haudenosaunee (ho-dee-noh-SHO-nee) A term for the people of the Iroquois Confederacy meaning "people of the longhouse."

hominy (HA-muh-nee) Hulled and dried kernels of corn that are boiled.

league (LEEG) A group that is united and that shares the same beliefs.

58

lodge (LAHJ)   Another name for a Haudenosaunee longhouse.

longhouse (LONG-hows)   A Haudenosaunee dwelling made of wood and elm bark. As the name suggests, a longhouse was long, having a door on both ends.

matrilineal (ma-truh-LIH-nee-uhl)   Tracing ancestral heritage through your mother's side of the family.

mimic (MIH-mihk)   To copy the actions or speech of someone else.

moccasin (MAH-kuh-suhn)   A Native American shoe made of strong leather and sometimes decorated with beads.

nation (NAY-shuhn)   A group of people who share the same beliefs and who follow the same laws.

orator (OR-uh-tuhr)   Someone known for his or her ability to speak well.

regalia (rih-GAYL-yuh)   Traditional Native American clothing, usually worn during ceremonies.

reservation (reh-zuhr-VAY-shuhn)   A piece of land set aside by the federal government on which Native Americans live.

sachem (SAY-chuhm)   A leader of a Native American nation.

sacred (SAY-kruhd)   Something that is considered holy.

sober (SOH-buhr)   Not under the influence of drugs or alcohol.

succotash (SUH-kuh-tash)   A Native American dish made from hominy and beans.

symbol (SIHM-buhl)   A word or an image used to represent an idea.

Glossary and Pronunciation Guide

treaty (TREE-tee)   An agreement between two people or groups.

wampum (WAHM-puhm)   A long belt or string made of white and purple shells. Wampum was used to record events and to bind contracts and was given as gifts of honor. Wampum was never used by Native Americans as currency.

Resources

BOOKS

Graymont, Barbara. *The Iroquois.* New York: Chelsea House, 1988.

Parker, Arthur C. *Parker on the Iroquois.* Syracuse, NY: Syracuse University, 1968.

Sneve, Virginia Driving Hawk. *The Iroquois.* New York: Holiday House, 1995.

Waldman, Carl. *Encyclopedia of Native American Tribes.* New York: Checkmark Books, 1999.

———. *Who Was Who in Native American History: Indians and Non-Indians from Early Contacts through 1900.* New York: Facts on File, 1990.

MUSEUM

New York State Museum
Empire State Plaza
Albany, NY 12330
(518) 474-5877
Web site: http://www.nysm.nysed.gov/iroquoisvillage
The New York State Museum has created a model Mohawk Iroquois village, depicting Iroquois life in the early seventeenth century.

61

WEB SITES

Due to the changing nature of Internet links, PowerKids Press has developed an online list of Web sites related to the subject of this book. This site is updated regularly. Please use this link to access the site:

www.powerkidslinks.com/lna/iroquois

Index

Index